Part 1 – How To Write & Upload Your Book

Table of Contents

Introduction

Welcome and thank you for purchasing my book, *Kindle Publishing Unveiled Box Set Write.Upload.Advertise.Sell* on Kindle and Generate a Six Figure Annual Passive Income.

Kindle Direct Publishing, or KDP, is a section from Amazon which allows *anyone* to publish an eBook and to make money online.

By going through this quick start guide, you will understand what it takes to write, sell, market, and generate passive income.

Now, let's get started.

Chapter 1: Why KDP?

I'm glad you asked.

Amazon is one of the biggest online retailers and it has an enormous potential in regard to online selling and marketing (physical products, books, etc.). For those who want to start an online business using this powerful engine, things might get interesting as time goes by.

What makes the difference?

When people are searching for something on Google, they don't necessarily look for something to purchase, but here comes the magic – when people are looking for something on Amazon, they are looking exclusively to buy something. Amazon has over 600 million credit cards in their database and this makes it unbeatable compared other platforms.

Kindle Direct Publishing (KDP) is an exclusive service from Amazon that allows *anyone* to self-publish his/her books and get money from them. I repeat – *Anyone* can publish a kindle eBook about any kind of niche. If you are wondering what this business requires, the answer is commitment, motivation, and good English skills.

You will tell yourself now that you are not a writer and you can't do something like that. You do not have to be a writer, you can hire someone to write the books for you, someone who uses your instructions and ideas. I'm sure you've seen a lot of fancy books on Amazon, a lot of them being written by famous authors and other books written by indie publishers (like you and I). You don't need to design an eBook cover for yourself, you can also hire a freelancer who can create a cover for you for $10.

You don't need to do all this by yourself, you need to hire people and outsource these tasks – you are an entrepreneur rather than a writer. I like to write my own books, but I like to give tasks such as proofreading, ghostwriting, or cover designing to others. I believe that my time is much more valuable than $10 for some tasks that may take more than 2 hours. Time is money, so be careful how you evaluate your time.

Chapter 2: How Does It Work?

Independently publish with Kindle Direct Publishing to reach millions of readers.

Get to market fast. Publishing takes less than 5 minutes and your book appears on Kindle stores worldwide within 24-48 hours.

Make more money. Earn up to 70% royalty on sales to customers in the US, Canada, UK, Germany, India, France, Italy, Spain, Japan, Brazil, Mexico, Australia and more. Enroll in KDP Select and earn more money through Kindle Unlimited and the Kindle Owners' Lending Library.

Keep control. Keep control of your rights and set your own list prices. Make changes to your books at any time.

Get started today! Publish your books with KDP. Learn how easy it is.

You just have to go to the www.kdp.amazon.com, create an account and complete all the required fields.

As soon as you finish completing all the fields, you can publish any book and however many books you want. You will now probably ask, "And what am I supposed to write about?" or "I'm not a writer, I can't do that." Oh, actually, yes, you can. Remember what I told you last chapter – *Anyone* can do it.

How? Here's the fun part – you have 2 big possibilities. You can write the book yourself, which I highly recommend in the beginning to make some cash and then to reinvest the money in hiring freelancers to help you out with all the time consuming tasks.

How much money can you earn?

It depends. You can earn $100 to $1,000,000 or even more. It depends on you, on what you want to publish, if you publish fiction or non-fiction books, the niches that you choose, on what markets you have, and also depends on the quality of the book and what you deliver to readers, if you give them the value you have promised in your title and description.

What should I write about to have success?

Write about whatever you like, but before you decide what to do, you should write about a topic that you already have knowledge about. The best books that you will create will be those about that which you have some knowledge about. If you know what you are talking about in a book, if you have experience and if you enjoy learning new things about that topic, then start writing.

Decide what you want to write about and then do *market research*.

Market research takes an hour or so to do and it's the most important part of your future success with KDP. If the topic that you have knowledge about also sells well on Amazon, then go ahead with it. In the next chapter, I will show you how to do market research properly.

Chapter 3: How to Do Market Research

This is the most important part of how you can make money on Kindle:

Let's see an example. You want to do some market research about... weight loss or diets. You need to go to "Kindle eBooks", then you choose the main category, which is "Health, Fitness and Dieting":

Show results for

New Releases
Last 30 days (4,394)
Last 90 days (14,689)
Coming Soon (525)

‹ Kindle Store
‹ Kindle eBooks
  Health, Fitness & Dieting
    Alternative Medicine (17,314)
    Beauty & Fashion (4,263)
    Death & Grief (5,454)
    Diets & Weight Loss (18,270)
    Disorders & Diseases (13,869)
    Exercise & Fitness (9,582)
    Mental Health (14,989)
    Nutrition (6,456)
    Personal Health (23,272)
    Psychology & Counseling (48,201)
    Recovery (3,707)
    Reference (967)
    Relationships (28,031)
    Safety & First Aid (1,076)
    Sex (6,181)

Refine by

Author
J. J. Virgin (2)
Susan Cain (1)
Mike Dooley (1)
Daniel Kahneman (1)
Dale Carnegie (4)
Dallas Hartwig (2)
Melissa Hartwig (2)
+ See more

Health, Fitness & Dieting

Recommended for You

Diabetes Cure: My Against All Odds.
Jessica Brennan, William Black...
☆☆☆☆☆ (10)
Kindle Price: **$10.53**
Why recommended?

Paleo Diet: 365 Days of Paleo Diet...
› Emma Katie
☆☆☆☆☆ (5)
Kindle Price: **$1.23**
Why recommended?

› See more recommendations

Best-selling Books in Featured Categories

Diets & Weight Loss
The Bulletproof Diet: Lose...
Dave Asprey, J.J. Virgin
10-Day Green Smoothie...
JJ Smith
Wheat Belly Total Health...
William Davis

You cannot publish a book that outranks all the other books. You can obviously see that there are thousands of books for each subcategory, so what you want to do is to go deeper into the other subcategories.

‹ Kindle Store
‹ Kindle eBooks
‹ Health, Fitness & Dieting
  Diets & Weight Loss
    Diets (17,512)
    Food Counters (1,003)
    Special Conditions (203)

We choose "Diets & Weight Loss" for the next subcategory and then we go further to "Diets" and then to "Weight Loss". Now there are no other many micro categories and notice that it is much easier to outrank 2,000 – 9,000 books than 200,000 or more.

‹ Kindle Store
‹ Kindle eBooks
‹ Health, Fitness & Dieting
‹ Diets & Weight Loss
‹ Diets
  Weight Loss

You need to look for certain keywords that people are searching all the time.

Include those keywords in your description, title, and subtitle and when they are required (I will cover this later on).

We have found all of the subcategories, so now you look for titles that others have and sell. You need to know what is selling the most. You go to kindle books and choose "Best Seller" and then you look after the category and subcategories you have already chosen. You will see top 100 paid and top 100 free.

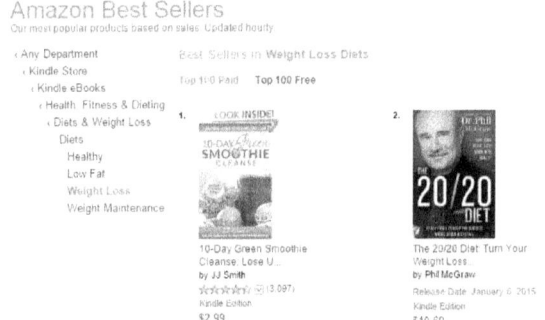

Then you want to click on some books and see what rank they have and how well are they selling these books with those titles.

Amazon Best Sellers Rank: #462 Paid in Kindle Store (See Top 100 Paid in Kindle Store)
#1 in Kindle Store > Kindle eBooks > Health, Fitness & Dieting > Diets & Weight Loss > Diets > **Weight Maintenance**
#1 in Kindle Store > Kindle eBooks > Health, Fitness & Dieting > Diets & Weight Loss > Diets > **Weight Loss**
#1 in Kindle Store > Kindle eBooks > Health, Fitness & Dieting > **Nutrition**

Would you like to **give feedback on images** or **tell us about a lower price**?

Amazon Bestseller's Rank shows how many copies the author sold in that day. Now you will think...hmm, isn't 462 a big number? NO! In fact, it's too good to be real. The lower the rank, the better it is and more sales you have. This book is ranked #462 in the whole Kindle store and in the Kindle store, there are over 3,100,000 books.

Amazon helps you see everything and it does all the marketing for you. You don't have to know anything about marketing. The book shows you what is selling best, that means #1 for the Weight

Maintenance category, #1 for Weight Loss, and #1 for Nutrition. There is a kdpcalculator, which tells you how much you sell by rank. At rank #462 paid in Kindle store, you sell 100 to 300 copies a day.

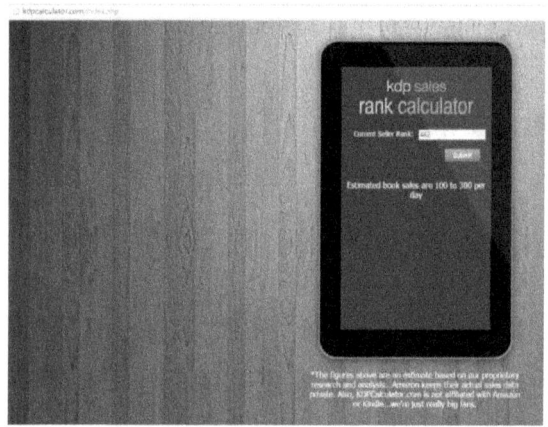

If you write a book in one of those Top Paid # subcategories, even if it's the last one, then congratulations, you are on your way to success.

So let's summarize:

1. Find out what topics you like.
2. You go to Kindle Store
3. You choose a niche
4. Choose category, subcategories, and micro categories
5. Do some market research, go to top #100 paid books in that category
6. Look for some titles and look at how good are they selling and figure out which is selling best
7. Find the best keywords in Amazon search bar and look at what market you have

Chapter 4: Starting Your Book

As soon as you finish doing market research and you choose a good and profitable niche, figure out a title, an eye catching title, a subtitle, with a lot of keywords. Do not make short titles like *Weight Loss Guide*. It's very bad, it doesn't suggest anything. Do something like *Extreme Weight Loss Bible – The Fastest Way to Lose Weight, Gain Your Health, and Live a Happy Life.*

I hope you got the idea. You include more keywords and it's easier to rank the book and it's even easier for buyers to find your book. The more keywords you have, the more readers you reach and the more money you make.

The book you want to write and make money with must have an original content, any copy from Google or other is plagiarism and you get into real trouble. So, make sure your book's content is 100% original. You can outsource it though, don't panic.

To sell a lot of books, create a lot of books, and make a lot of money, you need to focus on a few main things:

1. Books have to be short (15 – 80 pages), you can write longer ones, but you waste money and time.
2. You have to deliver what you have promised in the title (How to... swim... Well... teach them exactly how to swim)
3. Write a lot of these on the most profitable niches you find.
4. Repeat the first three.

Chapter 5: How Do I Write My Book?

You do not have to if you are not a writer. You may write the book by yourself if you want and you are good at writing, but be aware that an awful book with a lot of mistakes won't sell too much or for too long.

Where to go?

You have some options. You can go to http://freelancer.com but it's a little bit complicated, the fastest way and the best service, in my opinion, is http://iWriter.com

You can have books written for low prices, or if you want the ultimate quality content and you have money to invest, you can pay even more than $1,000 for a book.

Decide what chapters (titles) you want to add to your books, and give them to writers to write as articles, do not give them to write as a full length eBook. Why? They will charge you more!

If you want to write a book with 15 chapters (articles) with at least 1,000 words each, they will cost you $157.5 and you get 15,000–16,000 words, which is a book with 80-100 pages on Kindle (depending on the spacing, font size, if you have pictures, etc.)

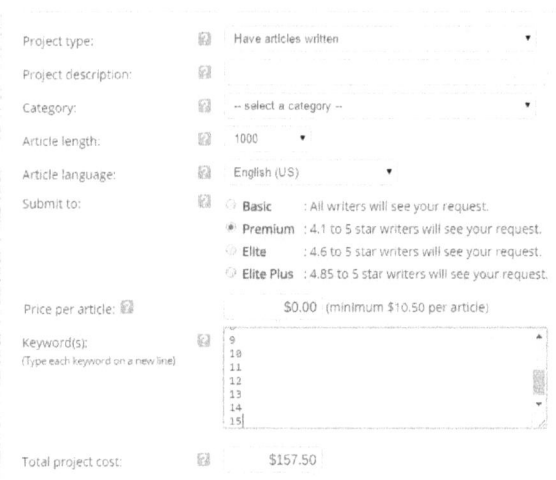

Project type:	⚡	Have articles written ▾
Project description:	⚡	
Category:	⚡	-- select a category -- ▾
Article length:	⚡	1000 ▾
Article language:	⚡	English (US) ▾
Submit to:	⚡	○ Basic : All writers will see your request.
		◉ Premium : 4.1 to 5 star writers will see your request.
		○ Elite : 4.6 to 5 star writers will see your request.
		○ Elite Plus : 4.85 to 5 star writers will see your request.
Price per article: ⚡		$0.00 (minimum $10.50 per article)
Keyword(s):	⚡	9
(Type each keyword on a new line)		10
		11
		12
		13
		14
		15
Total project cost:	⚡	$157.50

Now, to write an eBook with at least 7,000 words (mandatory), it requires you to pay at least $160. You pay even less for the previous method for which you get more than double in length.

Project type:		Have a Kindle book written ▾
Project description:		
Category:		Health and Fitness ▾
eBook length:		7.000 (~20 pages) ▾
Article language:		English (US) ▾
Submit to:		⦿ **Premium** : 4.1 to 5 star writers will see your request.
		○ **Elite** : 4.6 to 5 star writers will see your request.
		○ **Elite Plus** : 4.85 to 5 star writers will see your request.
Project price.		$0.00 (minimum $160.00 per article)
Chapter titles:		⦿ You choose the titles for the writer.
		○ Allow writer to make up their own titles.
Total chapters:		1 ▾

Now, don't worry, you do not have to pay anything to writers until you like the content, you can ask them to rewrite everything until you are satisfied with it.

Okay, so you give them the chapters, the titles, the instructions, you get your book done within 2-10 days, depending on how hard your writer works and how much work he has to do.

Before we move on to the next chapters, let me tell you something – if you want to do an outstanding job on Kindle, you need to be sure that the book you are about to write will be high quality, and it will deliver value to readers. With these qualities + the right advertising methods, you will dominate the market very quickly.

Chapter 6: How to Make Your Cover

There are 3 main ways to design your cover:

1. Design it yourself – Use photo editing software (such as Adobe Photoshop, for example, any other software is okay as well). Select or buy a stock image from www.fotolia.com or www.shutterstock.com and insert it in your future cover. The aspect ratio that Amazon requires for eBook is 1.6 – so a cover with the resolution of 1600x1000 pixels should be perfect. If you don't know Photoshop, you can learn it in a couple of months or you can use the next two alternative methods. If you are planning to design a cover that can also be used for CreateSpace, use a 6 x 9

inches format in Adobe Photoshop and select 300 dpi level.

2. Use Cover Creator within Amazon – it's free and easy to use. You have to put in a title, the author's name, and an image/background color. When you choose to do this, the cover that you create will be instantly uploaded.

3. Pay for your cover – You have multiple solutions (multiple websites and different levels of quality). You can have your book designed on www.99designs.com by premium designers. An eBook cover is $299 to $1,199 (from bronze to platinum level

designers – $299 bronze, $499 silver, $799 gold, or $1,199 platinum). You just tell them what you want in your cover, what they should follow, and you will get 30 to 90 premium designs from which you choose only one (it's a contest based design – a lot of designers enter the contest and you choose the best design).

You can also have your cover created on www.freelancer.com or other freelancing websites for a similar price.

If you want a really cheap cover that will be ready in less than 24 hours, go on www.fiverr.com and you will find a lot of designers there who make really nice designs for the money you pay. I usually pay $10-$20 for my cover on Fiverr and I get it done within 3 days. Some of the covers from my books are made by myself (these book covers are made by me).

I recommend you let the guys from http://Fiverr.com do that for you for only $5 (or $10-20 if you have any premium requirements). You get it 24 hours to 3 days later, depending how many people are in queue.

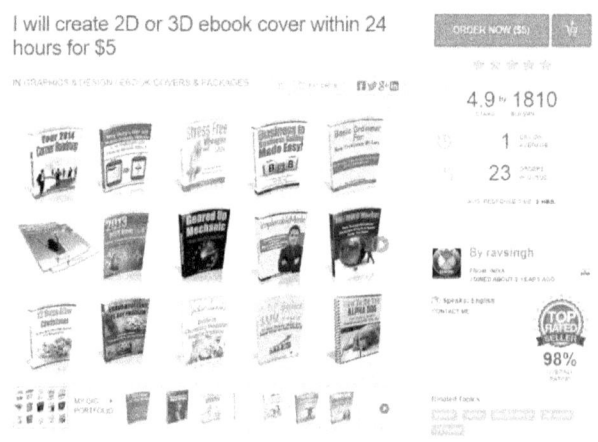

I worked with designers from Fiverr. They deliver the covers fast and you don't have to do any additional tasks.

Let them do them for you, I think $5 or so isn't worth the time to design the cover yourself and lose precious hours. If you don't have the money, or you want to use that money to promote your book, then do it yourself.

Chapter 7: Formatting the Book

As soon as you choose your niche and you do market research (see previous chapters), you can start writing your book. Use Microsoft Word for Windows or Pages for Mac OS.

Make sure to write an introduction, good quality content, a conclusion, and most important of all, a table of contents (TOC).

It's important to create a table of contents, as readers shouldn't have to scroll all the time to go to a specific chapter of a book because that would be really annoying for them. It's easy to do it, you just need to insert Bookmarks and Hyperlinks to the Bookmarks you create; there are a lot of tutorials on YouTube on how to do it. There are just

3 buttons to use – Insert -> Bookmark and Hyperlink (in Microsoft Word).

If you aren't too good at formatting a book or you do not want to waste time, you can go to www.Fiverr.com and let the guys format it and proofread your work (which somebody else did as well) for $5 or $10.

Make sure your content is clean. It provides valuable information to the readers and ensures you do not have any grammatical mistakes. Spelling mistakes are bad in any book and they must be avoided as much as possible even though there's no book in this world that doesn't have at least one mistake.

When you finish writing and formatting your book, you only have to upload it on Kindle and it will be automatically converted into the Kindle format from your .doc (Microsoft Word document format) or Pages format in just a couple of moments (it may take longer if you have pictures or such).

Chapter 8: Uploading Your Book

Now that you are done with your cover and content and you have formatted your book, you can upload it on Kindle.

Make sure you have an account. If you don't, sign up and let's get started. Before you can upload a book, you need to complete the tax information and make sure you have a credit card attached to the account. Unless you have these, you won't be able to continue to publish a book.

You go to www.kdp.amazon.com and then you go to your Bookshelf and click on "Add New Title". Now, what you have to do:
Tick the box with "Enroll in KDP Select".

KDP Select has two things to offer: Promotional free days (5 days every 90 days) for your book and also countdown deals and Kindle Unlimited, which offers users the ability to borrow your books for a limited period of time, for free. The good thing is that you receive a small sum, Amazon has a monthly fund for the whole number of books that are borrowed each month and depending on how many books you lend, the more you will get.

So make sure to tick that box.

Next, you enter your title, subtitle, you as an author. Use pen names, look for the most suitable pen names for the type of niche that you are posting in. Another important aspect is not to combine a lot of different niches for one pen name.

For example, choose a name like James Rodes for a health niche and John Taylor for a business niche. You are the publisher, the authors are the pen names you choose. It's indicated by Amazon to do so and not to confuse people.

"Hey, what am I buying here, a cookbook from an author who sells engineering books?"

It doesn't go well. So choose a pen name for every niche. (a general one, I hope you've got the point)

Choose your language (the language of the content from the book, probably English, but you can write in any language) and then tick below the "This is not a public domain" box. That means you have an original content that isn't someone else's work.

Now add the categories, the ones for which you have done the market research (they will be a little different here than the ones on the home page, choose the ones that are the closest to ones on the home page)

Upload your cover and then your content. As soon as you upload, it will tell you if you have spelling mistakes and it will tell you where you do if you have any. It may take longer to upload if you have images in your book content.

Then you click "Save and Continue" down below and move to the next one.

Then you choose the royalty options, which are 35% and 70% - you receive 35%. You can put a price between $0 and $200, but the range between $2.99 and $9.99 gets 70% royalty. In the beginning, you will choose $0.99 and I will explain why in the following chapter.

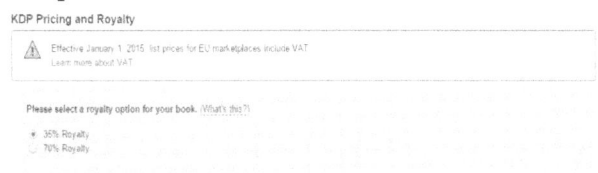

KDP Pricing and Royalty

Effective January 1, 2015, list prices for EU marketplaces include VAT
Learn more about VAT

Please select a royalty option for your book. (What's this?)

● 35% Royalty
○ 70% Royalty

Chapter 9: Promoting Your Book and Getting Your First Sales

Here's where you will be nervous and you can't wait to see some money coming from your book. I will honestly tell you that it takes two weeks to a month until you start making money passively and continuously, each month.

What you have to do:

Ask your family, friends, pay someone, or just wait to get some reviews. Your first reviews matter a lot to your book. As soon as you get between 5 and 10 reviews, you can go to your KDP account to KDP Select and set 1 to 5 days to make your book free (I recommend at least 3) – you will get a minimum of 50-100 downloads/day so for 3 days, you should get a minimum of 150-400 downloads (without any paid promotions).

Now, here's a small problem – that number of downloads isn't enough to make daily sales. You need to invest in advertising and there are hundreds of methods which I discussed in my second book, which is about how to promote your book.

http://www.amazon.com/Kindle-Publishing-Unveiled-Advertise-marketing-ebook/dp/B00RUAWW72/ref=sr_1_2?s=digital-text&ie=UTF8&qid=1422110873&sr=1-2&keywords=kindle+publishing+unveiled&pebp=1422110877570&peasin=B00RUAWW72

From those downloads, you may get some reviews, and from those downloads, you rank higher and will start to appear in Amazon's searches and people will start finding your book more easily, even when you are done with the free promotion days.

As soon as you finish this, your book is on autopilot for three months; it will generate passive income. Every three months, you need to promote your book again and to update it (if necessary). You will be surprised to see $10/month to up to $1,000/month or even more, depending on the niche, market, audience, and how well you advertise your book.

Advertising is crucial for any kind of product you want to sell – quality is also essential for long-term profits, but in the short-term, advertising is what will boost your sales and rankings. What I'm saying is try to combine quality with advertising and you will be surprised by the results.

There are a lot more details to cover here but I will present the basics and what you have to do ASAP to make money.

Join Twitter and Facebook groups, put links with your free book, and go to sites that host your book when it's free and boost your downloads on the free promotion trial. If you have a blog, website, or YouTube channel, use them to promote your book.

There are websites that charge $10 to $500 for one book, but they have proved to be highly effective. It's not wise to invest $500 in one single website. I like to go to different websites and invest around $150-$200 in 4-5 websites.

Chapter 10: Getting Paid

Everyone is very excited when they are releasing their first book or their first books. You won't see any sales in the first 2-3 weeks, so be patient. There's a whole process to do before that. It's natural not to receive any money in your first days and weeks because you are nowhere to find on Amazon; your book just got there and needs some attention.

If the book is good and someone is looking for that specific topic, you may sell your book without any reviews or without any advertising, but this happens very rarely.

If you do as I recommended in the previous chapters, to do market research, write your book, make a good cover, format your book, publish it, and choose good keywords, *then* what will really boost and send your book on the sales track will be to use the KDP Select free days and try to a minimum promotion on websites, Facebook groups, Fiverr, etc., to make additional downloads.

The more downloads you get, the higher you will rank for your title and keywords, and your book will show up higher in the searches. That's what you need, and sales will start to come after a month (of publishing).

The free promotion days can boost your sales for one book up to 500% and you are allowed to use 5 days every 90 days in KDP Select, so use them wisely.

How and when are you going to get paid by Amazon?

You will get paid every 60 days - Amazon sends you an email 10 days before the payment is processed (generally on the 20th every month) and you will receive the money at the end of the month or the start of the new month – 29th to 2nd (next month).

Tip – the money you earn from borrows (KOLL/KU units) are also paid on the same date, but you will see the reports for borrows in the "Prior Month Royalties" – Amazon sends you a report on 15th for the previous month and it will show you how much money you made from everything including borrows.

You will usually get from $1.35 to $1.5 for a borrow, depending on the number of borrows in total for that month. Notice that you will have a paid borrow if a customer who borrows your book has read at least 10% of the book. If a customer doesn't read at least 10%, you won't get paid (usually, almost all of the borrows are paid).

UPDATE 1st July 2015

The KU/KOLL system has been changed as a result of complaints of authors and I totally agree with the new system. Instead of being paid if at least 10% of your book is read, authors are now paid for every individual page that was read.

What does this mean? If you have a 20 page book, you will get paid for those 20 pages that a customer reads. If you are unlucky and the customer doesn't like your book, he/she will borrow your book, read 2 pages, and throw it away.

Before this update, everyone earned $1.35 for a borrow, no matter how long the book was. Now, a 20 page book will earn $0.2 (if fully read) if the price per page is $0.01. Similarly, if an author has a novel that has 500 pages, the author will earn $5 for a borrow (if the book is fully read).

In conclusion, writers who have less than 135 pages will earn less than before, writers who have 135 pages will earn the same, and writers who have lengthy books will earn more.

The number of pages will be calculated automatically by KENP (Kindle Edition Normalized Pages), so don't try to fool the system with big fonts and double spacing because it won't work.

Chapter 11: The Six Figure Recipe – Myth or Reality?

Now, I've presented how to write, publish, design, and promote your book. Now we are interested in getting a 6 figure annual passive income, aren't we?

A book (usually) generates $50 to $500, depending on a lot of factors (niche, content, title, value, number of pages, price, etc.). Now, think – how many books do you need and how much time does it take to reach over $100,000/year?

Here is the answer:

Write one book a month – Spend time working on your book each day. In the two weeks, write it yourself or get content for your book, arrange all your ideas, and create the content. During the 3rd week, focus on polishing the details of your book – proofread, cover, formatting, and other minor details. In the 4th week, make sure to promote it.

If you do all of these properly, you will be able to generate at least $200 from a single book, every single month, but be sure to promote it again every three months. To grow this Kindle Publishing business, you need to permanently improve yourself, your books, and to invest money.

Now, you will not have the same results for each book. You will have one that makes $1,000/month, two that make $50/month, and five that make $200/month – you will ever know exactly how much money you will make and every month is different (regarding sales). If you create one book a month and you make in average $300/book, in one year, you will be able to generate around $3,600/month, after two years, $7,200, and after three years, $10,800/month.

You will never be able to reach these numbers without a blog, a YouTube channel, paid advertising, and a *lot* of work on a daily basis. Anyone who tells you that being an online entrepreneur, an author, or a freelancer is easy doesn't know what they're talking about. The only things what make this business very attractive are:

1. It is scalable – You control it and you can grow it without any limits.
2. You obtain profits very quickly – This is probably the fastest method to make money online (as far as I'm concerned,

it's the fastest method I personally know).

Okay, so after three years of hard work, you will be able to generate $10,800, but you won't get $10,800 net profit. You will be paying a withholding tax from 10 to 30% (depending on if you are a resident of U.S. or non-U.S. resident), you will need to invest at least 20% of the money you earn (advertising, content, blog, virtual assistant, etc.). Out of $10,800, which is $129,600 gross income, from which you pay 15% as a U.S. resident, 30% as a non-U.S. resident, or 10% if you are a non-U.S. resident but the country in which you live is in tax treaties with U.S. (my case). This is available only for sales made in the U.S. store (which are 80-90% of your total sales). In the other stores, you don't pay any withholding taxes, but you pay VAT (for EU).

Let's say you pay 15%, for 85% of that $129,600 – you will need to pay 15% tax for $110,160, which is $16,524. Y + our total amount of money remaining is ($110,160 – $16,524 + $19,440 (sales made on the other stores for which withholding taxes are not applied) so you will be making $113,076 net income, but you need to invest at least 20% in advertising and other services to grow and maintain your income – $22,615. So your final remaining amount of money per year after three years of hard work will be $90,480. If you push hard one more year, you will exceed $100,000 per year net income, but you need to be very serious with yourself and you need to be dedicated to this business.

If you are lucky enough, you will probably reach those number faster, but

I believe that no matter what you do, as an indie publisher, you won't be able to reach a 6 figure annual income in less than 2 years. This isn't a 'get rich scheme', it's a business that requires work and dedication.

You just manage all these tasks and tell other people what to do for you. A freelancer creates a cover, another one creates the content, and another one promotes it. You just take everything and put them all together and wait for your sales to come by.

The only condition here is if you really want to achieve this goal. Even if it sounds easy, it isn't that easy, but it's a lot easier than other ways to make money.

PART 2 – How To Promote Your Book

Table of Contents

Introduction

In this book, you will learn:

- How to promote your book
- What readers are looking for
- Where to promote your book
- What helps your book to sell
- How to use Amazon's promotional tools
- How to choose a good title
- How to increase your sales

Chapter 1: Why it is Important to Promote Your Book

No matter who you are and what product you create, whether it's physical or digital, advertising is one of the major players in increasing profits (in our case, sales). No matter how hard you work to make a high quality product, if you do neglect advertising, your future profits will suffer or even die.

In some cases, product developers have released products that are okay, not even close to the word "quality", but they have invested thousands of dollars in advertising and people started to buy that product just because it's "popular" or because it's a new "trend".

Applying this principle into our case, a book that isn't advertised won't do well.

All the bestselling books on Amazon are bestselling because of 2 factors:

1. The author is very popular and it doesn't need any additional advertising for books on Kindle (even if he invested money in his public image before being popular).
2. As an indie publisher (totally unpopular), you pay for advertising your books among other free methods.

How can you promote your books?

Here's a short comprehensive list:

1. Free websites
2. Paid advertising
3. Promote on Social Media platforms (again – free or paid)
4. Creating a blog to engage readers and to bring traffic to the blog and

then again to the other books (or products)

5. Creating a YouTube channel with dedicated videos for every book
6. Creating a Cross-Promotion series within each book – every book that you have has a chapter at the end that promotes another book of yours. Book A promotes book B, book B promotes book C, book C promotes book D, and so on.

7. Creating an email list from your blog – every time you release a new book, send an email to your followers and encourage them to download and read it by offering them freebies.

Before you start promoting your book, make sure that you do the most important thing of all – Sign up with KDP Select. Without this service, you will only be able to promote your book by dropping the price to $0.99, but you will be limited.

First, I highly recommend to enroll in KDP Select and to give away your book for 5 days every 90 days.

Chapter 2: KDP Promotional Tools

Kindle knows that authors need help to get promoted as fast as possible and Amazon is also directly interested in your sales – the more sales you get, the bigger the profits are for you and Amazon. In other words, you and Amazon depend on each other.

So, Amazon has its own promotional tools, which are:

1. **KDP Select - Free Promotional Days** – You are allowed to promote your book for 5 days every 90 days only if you agree to post exclusively your book on Kindle. What this does is that it offers your book for free for up to 5 days – you can set 24 hours, or 2, 3, 4, or 5 days. It's

your choice on how many days you want to promote it. I tried to promote my books for 3 days or 5 days and the best period to do this is from Sunday to Thursday – it just gets the biggest amount of downloads. When people download your book, your book will automatically rank higher and it will be easier for readers to find your book. The principle is easy: more downloads => higher rank => more sales after the free promotion => more profit.

Step 1	Step 2	Optional
Your book	Rights & Pricing	KDP Select Benefits
✓ Finished and available for purchase	✓ Published	

Run a price promotion for your book on Amazon

Create a new promotion

Sign your book up for one of the following promotional programs:

Only one promotional program can be enabled per enrollment period. Please select either Kindle Countdown Deals or Free Book Promotion.

| Free Book Promotion ▼ | Create a new Free Book Promotion Deal for this book. Learn more |

Promotions for this book

Promotion Type	Marketplace	Start	End	Duration	Status
Free Book Promotion		December 27, 2014	December 29, 2014	3 day(s)	Complete

2. **KDP Select – Countdown deals** – If you already have a paperback book or you have a very good quality book and you do not want to give it away for free, you can use the countdown deals – you set a base price, and it will rise every day during the 5 days. You are also allowed 5 days every 90 days but you have to choose wisely between free promo days and countdown deal days. There are 5 in total, not 5 for each.

As you can see here, I cannot use countdown deals until the 90 day period ends because I have already chosen to use Free Promo days.

3. **KDP Select – Kindle Unlimited –** You allow your readers to borrow your book and you reach a lot more readers. Don't worry, you get paid as well for borrowed units. This is also available when you enroll in KDP Select program.

The principle is simple. Amazon has a Prime membership currently available for US customers. For a Prime membership, you pay $100/year and you get a lot of benefits such as free shipping for a lot of products, rushed shipping, a lot of features for Amazon Fire TV, free TV programs, as well as an instant access to more than 700,000 books enrolled in KDP Select – Kindle Unlimited. There is a Global Fund each month for Kindle Unlimited and Kindle Online Lending Library (KOLL), in which also I recommend you to enroll in.

The Prime Membership is available only for the US, but there are some countries (Amazon marketplaces where you can have your book borrowed with Kindle Unlimited – customers pay 9.99$/month to borrow books (they have a limited number of borrows for each month).

KU/KOLL has recently become so popular, that now over 40% of the royalties that an author earns are from borrows, so make sure you have already allowed your books to be borrowed. The Global Fund is constantly growing, so more and more customers are likely to join this program.

Borrowed units are marked with a blue line in your dashboard sales like in the picture below:

To summarize this, all you need to know is that KU/KOLL helps you get more sales, more readers, and more money. On average, you get about $1.5/borrow if at least 10% of the borrowed book is read. Usually, most of the borrows are paid, there is very little chance for a person who borrows a book to ignore it or not to read it at all.

4. Amazon Sales Promotion – you get promoted by Amazon after you get a few sales or free downloads (which, in the end, count as sales) by showing your book to other readers – "Customers who bought this, also bought ..."

This helps you reach more readers and get more sales. Amazon does everything for you, all you need to do is wait for the first sales to come.

The same mechanism is for books that have just been viewed – "Customers who viewed this, also viewed…"

5. Bestsellers Rank for Categories and Subcategories – The better you sell your book, the more the book will be promoted by Amazon. You will get into some ranks, at first, in smaller subcategories, and the more sales you get (every day), the better your paid rank and so you will get in the Top #100 of the category the book is put into.

UPDATE 1st July 2015

As a result of the response of authors to the new Kindle Unlimited program, Amazon has decided to change the way they pay authors for loans.

The way Amazon paid authors before 1st July 2015:

If a reader borrows a book and reads at least 10% of the book, a royalty will be paid to the author ((Global Fund + Supplements)/Total Number of Borrows) = $1.35 - $1.5/borrow. This means that whether if you have a book of 10 pages or a book of 400 pages, if someone reads 10% (1 page – or just open the book for the 10 page book, or 40 pages for the 400 page novel) you earn the same royalty, which wasn't fair and encouraged scammers to create short "scamphlets" (scam + pamphlet).

The way Amazon is paying authors after 1ˢᵗ July 2015:

Amazon has decided to redistribute the way they are paying authors. They chose to pay each individual read page. This means that if you have 20 pages, you will be paid for those 20 pages, if you have a 400 page novel, you be paid for 400 pages (if it's fully read).

I just had a look at Amazon and there are over 1,000,000 titles enrolled in KDP Select, from which over 300,000 have less than 30 pages (150,000 have from 1 to 11 pages), so what will happen is this – authors who have books with less than 100-140 pages will earn the same money as before the change (if the book is fully read), authors who have books with less than 100 pages will lose money and authors who have lengthy books with 150

– 500 pages will earn a lot more money than before.

The new system encourages authors to write quality and lengthy books that engage readers. The main authors who will suffer will be scammers, but unfortunately, authors who write Children's Books will also suffer because of the short length. However, images and any graphic content will count as "pages".

The system that counts these pages is the Kindle Edition Normalized Pages (KENP) software.

Chapter 3: The Importance of Keywords

A lot of people do not give too much importance to keywords, but believe it or not, they are responsible for more than 50% of your sales, if they are chosen correctly. A keyword isn't just a word, it's something people are looking for, a small phrase. "How to write a book" for example. You are allowed to choose a maximum of 7 keywords similar to the example I gave you and you have to separate them by a coma.

Now, to choose the best keywords, you have to use Amazon's Search Bar and see what people are looking for. This is a very powerful tool and by using it correctly, you will choose the best keywords that have the biggest number of readers. The more readers you get, the more sales you get, simple as that.

I just typed "how to" and some suggestions appear – the first one has the biggest number of readers, then comes the second, the third, and so on. Depending on what you are writing about, you can choose the best keywords.

But wait, there is another trick to keep in mind. If the keyword is too broad and it has many thousands of results, your book will not be able to outrank those thousands. I mean, it can, but it's almost impossible. On the other hand, if the keyword is too narrow, you will not have too many results, which means not too many people are looking for the keyword you have chosen.

Let's look at some examples, so I can be sure that you got the idea. If I type "how to write a book" I will get 3,436 results so it will be very difficult, nearly impossible, to outrank 3,436 books, so your book will appear on the first page. In other words, the keyword is too broad. Let's go further.

If I type the keyword "how to write the book fast", I will get 101 results, so the keyword is too narrow, there are not enough results and not enough audience.

If I write "how to write and sell a book" I will get 294 results, so it's much better – you will be able to outrank 294 books with a free promo, if used correctly (I will cover how to get more free downloads in the next chapters).

This is just an example. I hope you've got the idea. Try to find the keyword that yielded between 300 and 1,000 results. I think the perfect number is around 500 results, so pick up to 7 keywords with about 500 results (the keywords should be similar or relevant to the title of your book or at least to the content of the book).

Keywords will help you get more free units, more sales, more money, and they will help you rank higher in the searches. And if the book is okay, Amazon will promote it even more. This is essential for the future of your Kindle Books so do not neglect them.

Chapter 4: Reviews

The reviews of a product tell you everything about it. The more reviews, the better it is for your book. The better reviews you get (above 4 / 5 rating), the more sales you get.

People generally judge a product by the cover (or aspect) and the reviews, so this becomes a very important aspect that you may want to take care of by putting the best book you can on Amazon. Every negative review will affect your sales (negatively).

It's difficult to make the first reviews, but by putting your book for free for a number of days, you will get some downloads and some people will take some time to review your book. But in some cases, they don't. The conversion rate is somewhere around 1 review/1,000 free downloads and 1 review/100 purchases. If you get more than that, you are lucky.

When a customer sees a book that has 400 reviews with an overall rating of 4 – oh, my God, I think this book is great and some of them buy it without looking at the sample, page count, or description. Because of this, scammers still survive on Amazon with 5 page books with 50 reviews (fake reviews). They won't be surviving for too long though, and I will tell you why.

On Kindle, you will see books that have over 50 reviews, from which 40 are of 5 stars, and they have 15 pages (full of crappy content with mistakes). In that case, most of the reviews are fake and it's visible from space that the author is trying to artificially raise his ranking and overall rating.

There is nothing wrong with a book that has 5-6 reviews from friends or family just to boost the sales a little bit or to make them start faster, but some authors love to game the system. Unfortunately for them, Kindle came out with the KENP software and they are restricting reviewers severely by flagging their accounts and deleting the reviews one by one.

On Amazon, there are 2 types of reviews: verified purchase reviews, which appears when a customer has downloaded or purchased a book and unverified reviews, which anyone can give an unverified review (most of these reviews come from haters - 1 star reviews or from people who borrow your book and want to write a review).

Negative Reviews

If you release a product or you write a book and you get a negative review, don't panic, it's natural - every single author gets negative reviews on Amazon, even if it's the best book in the world. Some of the comments may be true, but in most of the cases, people write a negative review without justifying their review. You will see reviews like "yawn" or "nope" or "neah" without specifying what they didn't like.

Chapter 5: Promoting Your Book on Websites

It's important to promote your book for your free promo days/countdown deal days to maximize your downloads, and then to get more sales. I will focus now on giving you suggestions on how to promote your book for the free promo days.

Here is a list of websites where you can submit your book. Some of them require a fee to subscribe your book, but they guarantee that they will promote your book accordingly.

Some of the websites are free and some of the websites charge you a fee, and they will promote your book in different places.

www.pixelofink.com

www.bargainbookhunter.com

www.thatbookplace.com

www.ebookshabit.com

www.freebookshub.com

www.ebooklister.com

www.ebooksfreedaily.com

www.frugalfreebies.com

www.onehundredfreebooks.com

www.snicklist.com

www.daily-free-ebooks.com

www.addictedtoebooks.com

Now here's a list with the best paid websites that I've used so far and which I highly recommend you to use for your future books:

For free promotion ($0.00)

- Bookbub
- ENT (ereadernewstoday)
- Freebooksy
- BKnights (Fiverr)
- DigitalBookToday
- BooksButterfly
- BookSends
- BookGorilla
- eBookshabit
- BookTweeters

From this list, I could say that BookBub is by far the best service for promoting a book - you can get 4,000 to 50,000 downloads during the free promotion, but prices are a little high - from $60 to $400 for a book depending on the genre and category. BookBub has its own requirements - you need to have a minimum number of pages, reviews, you need a premium cover and content that has been edited professionally.

Freebooksy is $50 - $100 depending on the genre and it promises somewhere between 1,000 and 7,000 (big numbers come from fiction books).

DigitalBookToday is very good and affordable - for $15 - $50 you can get outstanding results. They have a dedicated category for books that have been recently released.

eBookshabit - They send an email with your book to their subscribers (over 300,000) for $10 and you can get 200 – 1,000 downloads.

ENT - For $25, you can exceed 1,000 downloads easily, but unfortunately, you have to wait a while until you get approved and you have to wait until they schedule you. A slow, but good service.

BooksButterfly guarantees you a minimum number of downloads (NO BOTS). I used their service and they exposing the book to different websites and blogs. If you pay more, will expose your book to websites with higher traffic numbers. You can pay from $50 to $300.

BKnights is a gig from Fiverr who will provide you 100 to 800 downloads for only $5 - the best service for that price. I always use it.

Websites for promoting books at $0.99:

- BargainBooksy
- BuckBooks
- BookSends
- BooksButterfly

About BuckBooks

If there is a service that I can highly recommend to boost your rank, sales, and make some money during the promotion, then try BuckBooks. It's free for authors, but you need a high quality book with at least 40 pages or 10,000 words to get accepted. The cover needs to be clean and you should also have some good reviews for the book (not mandatory).

My results with BuckBooks for one of my books:

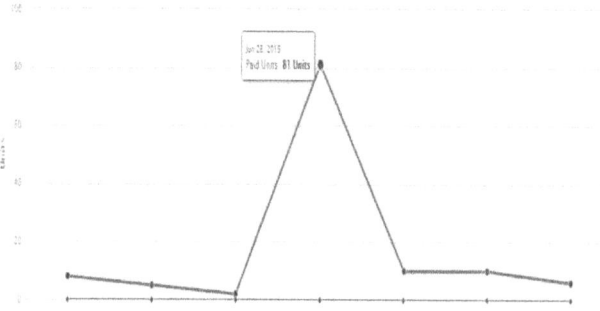

I got those purchases at $0.99 in one day - they don't guarantee you anything, but they told me that I should be expecting between 50 and 200 purchases.

In case you don't have time or you just want to sit more comfortable, you can go to www.Fiverr.com and you can also pay from 5$ to 40$ a gig to promote your book on websites.

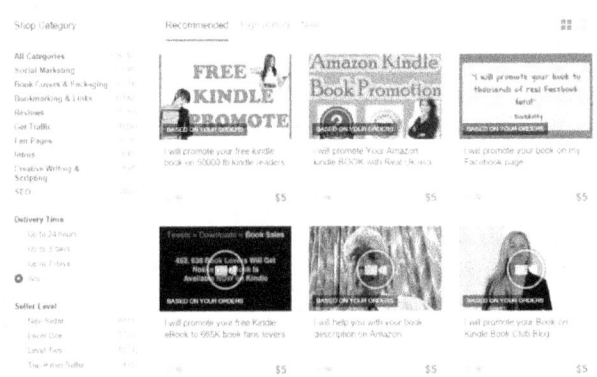

Chapter 6: Promoting Your Book on Facebook

Facebook is one of the largest social media websites on which people spend their time every day. Everyone does it, even me and even you, so let's use this powerful tool.

There are a lot of ways to promote your book on Facebook:

1. Creating a Fan Page for your book, or for you, as an author – Put the Fan Page link at the end of every book, people will start following you, so you will get more sales for your upcoming books. You can then promote your Fan Page on other websites as well.

2. Facebook Promote – Pay Facebook to advertise your book/your fan

page – It will help you get more traffic.

3. Use hashtags – Try to post your book on Facebook and use hashtags. Here is a small list of hashtags you may use: #freekindle, #freeebook, #kindle, #KDP, #freebook, #amazon, #goodreads, #freereads, #freestuff, etc. Try to use other ones of your own. Your book will get posted on those hashtags and people will see it.

4. Join Kindle Readers Groups – When you have a book to share or to promote, post it there and tell everyone that you will have a book that will be free. This helps a lot to boost your downloads for the book you want to promote.

Again, if you want your book to be promoted without any effort, go on Fiverr and order a promotion on Facebook (it's based on number 4 – they will promote your book to Kindle Readers secret groups of over 100,000 people or so)

Chapter 7: Promote Your Book on Twitter and Other Social Media Networks

Twitter is also a large social media site you can use to promote your book. Here is a list of where you can go and submit your free book to get additional downloads:

@kindlefreebooks

@kindle_free

@freeebooksdaily

@free2kindle

@pixelofink

@digitalinktoday

@kindlestuff

@kindlenews

@ebook

@free

@freeebookdeal

@freebookdude

@FreeKindleStuff

@IndieKindle

@KindleFreeBook

@KindleBookKing
@KindleUpdates

@Kindle_promo

@Kindledaily

There are a lot of social media networks where you can promote your book, just set up new accounts on Instagram, Pinterest, LinkedIn, Vimeo, etc. There are tons of places where people socialize every day.

Chapter 8: Set Up an Author Central Account

Setting an account on Author Central will help you get access to a lot more readers, people will be able to follow you (subscribe) and they will be notified when you have something new.

People will get the chance to know you better, to read your biography, which will give you better credibility and your sales will increase.

There also statistics there, the rank of the author on Amazon, so you have some other advantages there.

To set up your Author Central Account, go to www.authorcentral.amazon.com

Chapter 9: Pen Names

It's important to have different pen names for different niches that you write about because people get confused when they see one name for different niches. How would it look if I were write under the same pen name, or even my real name, in subjects like mathematics, cookbooks, engineering, diseases, food recipes, automotive, erotic novels, and children's books, all under the same name? Won't you get annoyed? Choose a pen name for one category like health, fitness and dieting, another pen name for business and money, and so on.

By choosing a pen name and posting books on a similar niche, you will become a "local expert" and people who like one of your books will click on your name, will read your biography, and will look at what other books you have for sale.

Chapter 10: Use Box Sets (Bundles)

If you have already posted 2 books that bind well together, or if you have a series of books, combine them 2 in 1. It's very profitable for you and it's also better for readers, they will pay less (that's the point of bundles).

This is just an example, you can use 3in1, 4in1, 5in1, 100in1, however many you like. I usually like to use 2in1 or 3in1. It's enough, I think.

If you have 2 books, and each has 30-50 pages and costs $2.99, instead of selling them at $5.98 separately, you can lower the price to $3.99 or $4.50 for both books.

If you have the books, you only have to make a different cover in which both books are included.

Chapter 11: Title and Subtitle

The title of your book and the subtitle are as important as the keywords. So, how do you make a good title?

1. First of all, describe the BENEFITS that the readers get from your book in the title. You should have at least 1 benefit in your titles, 2 are recommended. The more, the better.
2. The title should be long and descriptive.
3. It has to contain keywords in it, like the ones I showed you above – something like "how to". Use Amazon's search bar to figure out a nice title.
4. Even if the subtitle is optional, make descriptive subtitles and also

try to include a benefit or a keyword.

5. Include your book in a series of books, you will reach more readers as well.

Example of a good title – *Kindle Publishing Unveiled – How to Write, Promote, Market, and Sell Your Book – The Easiest and Fastest Way to Profit on Kindle*

As you can see, I have benefits – obtain profit on kindle fast and easy and I also have keywords – how to write, how to sell, how to market, how to promote your book.

Conclusion

Kindle is a gold mine and there are few people who know about this. It's continually evolving all over the world as people are now consuming a lot more information online and on their tablets, laptops, PCs, smartphones. And, it's natural to do so, it's more efficient, it's a lot faster, and you can keep with you on the go, providing unlimited content on your tablet. An eBook has less than 1-2 MB size. If you don't agree, please go ahead and carry 10-15 pounds of paper in your backpack.

It's a lot faster. You do not deliver the book from USA to Europe or vice-versa, you just click buy or download and it's delivered almost instantly. No more taxes, no more killed trees, no more high taxes and commissions. This is the future, the future is digital and it expands in that way. Old paper books will become history a few years from now.

If this book has been useful to you, please be kind and write a short review about what you think, I would be more than grateful if you want to share your thoughts with me.

Kindest Regards

www.ingramcontent.com/pod-product-compliance
Lightning Source LLC
Chambersburg PA
CBHW070908180526
45168CB00005B/1975